KNOWLEDGE

INCREASING KNOWLEDGE

AMRUTHA PHALA VALLI

I DEDICATE THIS BOOK TO MY DAUGHTER K.L.SUMA
VALLI, AND IT IS COMLETED BY THE COOPERATION OF
MY FAMILY MEMBERS

Contents

Foreword

LOOSING IS VICTORY POSPOTENED. WORLD WILL
FORGIVE FAILURE BUT WILL NOT FORGIVE PEOPLE
WHO HAVE UTILIZED THE OPPORTUNITIES.

Acknowledgements

FIRST OF ALL WE WOULD LIKE TO THANK MY OFFICE MEMBERS, FAMILY MEMBERS, PARENTS WHO HAVE GIVEN ALL SUPPORT AND ENCOURAGEMENT

Prologue

This book contains an introduction of the knowledge which is used in every field.

KNOWLEDGE

The fact or condition of knowing something with familiarity gained through experience or association is the knowledge

Knowledge can be defined as awareness of facts or as practical skills; and may also refer to familiarity with objects or situations. Knowledge facts also called proportional knowledge is often defined as true belief that is distinct from opinion or guesswork by virtue of justification.

TYPES OF KNOWLEDGE

What are the types of knowledge?

1. Explicit knowledge
2. Implicit knowledge
3. Tactic knowledge
4. Procedure knowledge
5. Declarative knowledge

EXPLICIT KNOWLEDGE

Explicit is the knowledge covering topics that are easy to systematically document and share out at scale; what we think of a structured information, when explicit knowledge is well managed, it can help a company make better decisions, save time and maintains and increase in performance.

These types of explicit knowledge are all things that have been traditionally been what has been captured in a knowledge base or a part of knowledge management strategy. It is a formulized documentation that can be used to do a job, make decisions, or inform an audience.

IMPLICIT KNOWLEDGE:

Implicit knowledge is essentially, learn skills or know how. It is gained by taking explicit knowledge and applying into a specific situation. If explicit knowledge is a book in the mechanics of flight and a lay out diagram of an airplane cockpit, implicit knowledge is what happens when you apply that in order to fly the plane.

Implicit knowledge is gained when you learn the best way to do something. You can take when you learn the best way to do something. You can take that experience and synthesize it with other learned information in order to solve an entirely new problem.

This type of knowledge has traditionally been excluded from formal knowledge bases, as it can be difficult to document and capture in a scalable way. In order to add it to all knowledge base, think of this way. What new thing did I learn, would it be useful to others.

TACTIC KNOWLEDGE

Tacit knowledge is the knowledge that we possess that is generated by personal experience and context. It is the information that, if asked would be the most difficult to write doubt, articulate or present in a tangible form. This can include personal wisdom, experienced, experience, insight and intuition.

Tacit knowledge since it is irreplaceable Competitors can take your tools and methods, but they cannot reproduce the contribution and experience of

your workers. So building a tacit knowledge base system is very important.

PROCEDURE KNOWLEDGE

Procedure knowledge refers to the knowledge of how to perform a specific skill or task and is considers related to methods, procedures or operation of equipment. Procedure knowledge is also referred to as implicit knowledge or know how.

DECLARATIVE KNOWLEDGE

Declarative knowledge refers to fact information stored in the memory that is considered static in nature. Declarative knowledge, describes things events or process; their attributes and their relation to each other.

1.THIS BEGINS A NEW PRACTICE

Knowledge is beyond events. Every event colors your awareness. In some way, pleasure, pain, joy, sorrow, anger, jealous etc. Each event gives a false notion of what reality is. Truth is beyond all the colors of particular events. Real knowledge is to know the extent of one's ignorance. Knowledge is power. Information is liberating. Education is the premise of progress, in every society, every family. Without knowledge action is useless and knowledge without action is futile.

Knowledge is something that will serve you your whole life. The fact or condition of knowing something with familiarity gained through experience or association. Knowledge is acquaintance with, understanding of a science, art or techniques.

2.ONLY SPEAK KNOWLEDGE; FIND COMFORT IN CONFLICTS

Only speak knowledge. Don't repeat anything bad that someone tells you about someone. And don't listen to someone who tells you that "so and so" told "such and such "about you. When someone tells you such things, discourage them. Don't believe it. Conflicts the nature of the world, comfort is the nature of the self.

When you are tired of conflicts and the games of the world, get into the comfort of the self. When you are bored with comfort get into the games of the world of the self. When you're bored with comfort, get into games of the world. If you are one of the masters close ones, you do both simultaneously.

3. MASTER IS THE DOOR

You are lost on the street. There is rain, thunder, wind and cold; you need shelter. You look around and you find a door. You come to door because it is more charming, more joyful than anything out on the street.

When you enter the door of the master, you come home. You see the world from a new perspective. From inside you can still hear the thunder and see the rain, but it take no longer disturbs you. Inside there is warm and security. The world looks much more beautiful –not a nasty place. It is filled with love, cooperation. Your fear drops away.

4.DOUBT

A doubt is a gray area. Gray is something which is neither black nor whiter. Now how to solve a doubt.

Accept a doubt as either black or white. See your doubt as white and there is no doubt. See the doubt as black and accept it. Either way you accept it and move on.

See someone as their honest or dishonest and accept him. Then you are not in the gray area of doubt. You have conviction. "he is dishonest and yet he is part of him" Accept him as he is.

Doubt is an unstable state with footing neither on the shore nor on the shore. From there tension arises one way or the other. Take a direction and regain your footings.

Have you noticed that you usually doubt only the thing that are positive in your life? Negative thoughts that you don't doubt. You doubt a person's honesty, and you believe in his dishonesty. When someone is angry with you, you have no doubt about his angry. But when someone says he loves you, a doubt creeps in. Does he really love me? When you are depressed, do you ever think "iam depressed" No you take depression as a fact. Yet when your happy, you doubt that you are capable, But do you ever doubt that you incapable.

5. HABITS AND VOWS

How to get rid of impressions? This is a question for all those who want to come out of habits. Because they give pain and restrict you. The nature of impression is to bother you, and wanting to be free is the nature of life.

What are some vows to say?

"I promise to never lose our spark and to always dothe little things to make you happy"

"I will always love you no matter what"

" I will promise to always make you laugh and to laugh together"

" I vow that we will be a family together ,for ever"

" I will never get bored when Iam with you"

How do you end a vow? A vow should be time bound. For eg, Suppose someone says, "I will quit smoking " but cannot do it. He can take a time bound vow not to smoking for five days. If someone is used to cursing and swearing; He can take a vow in not using bad language for ten days. Don't take a vow for a life time. You will break it immediately. If you happen to break it any time, don't worry ; just begin again . Slowly increase the length of your vow until it becomes your very nature.

6.DEALING WITH BLAME

When someone blames, what do you do usually? You blame them back or you put up a resistance in yourself.

How do you feel when someone blames you? Hurt, sad, heavy.? This is all because you are resisting. What you resist will persists. You get hurt because you resist the blame.

Know that when someone blames you, they take away some negative karma from you. If you understand this, you will be only be happy inside.

1. Critically examine the thought that you are being blamed for everything
2. Reach out to a trusted confident to help you sort out your thoughts and feelings.
3. Consider ways to avoid toxic relationship like in the future.
4. Take time for introspection
5. Take a critical look at the person giving the blame.
6. Speak with them about your concerns
7. Maintain healthy boundaries,

7.THE BIG MIND

You know that there is big mind and a small mind. Sometimes big mind wins over the small mind, sometimes it is other way around when the small mind wins, it is misery; when the big mind wins it is joy. The small mind promises joy and leaves your hand empty. The big mind may bring resistance in the beginging and later fills you with joy.

8.FREEDOM AND DISCIPLINE

Freedom and disciple are opposites. They are also complimentary. They are both active, internal processes developed through the child's own activity and effort. Freedom is the capacity to choose and discipline is the capacity to act on that choice. Freedom means being able to choose what is good for oneself. Discipline is the inner awareness and control over ones reconciliation between ones need and environment's need. Without discipline, a person is ultimately unable to do what he wants.

A very important problem in respect of integral education arises from its insistence on proper synthesis between freedom and discipline. Since education is an important process, and since compulsion and creativity cannot go together, freedom has to be a very important instrument of education.

Freedom means being able to choose what is good for onself. All people want what is good for themselves, yet freedom, also comes with responsibility. Children need the guidance and patience of the adults around them to develop self discipline.

9.HOW TO MAINTAIN INTIMACY

What breaks intimacy?

Ego or takes a position

Desire

Taking intimacy for granted

Finding imperfection in one selves or others

Take a critical look at the person giving the blame

Speak with them about your concerns

Maintain healthy boundaries

Expectation

Insensitivity or over sensitivity

Discretion or dispassion

Judgement

Grumbling or lack of gratitude

10.OVERCOMIG EVENTS

All the problems that you face in life are because you attach over importance to events. The events grow bigger while you remain smaller. Say for example you are riding a motor cycle on a busy street and in front of you another vehicle is emitting exhaust fumes. You have three options

You can complain, somehow bear with and still follow the vehicle

You can slow down or wait for wait for some time to allow the vehicle to more far away from you.

You can use your skill, over take the vehicle, and forget about it.

As in the first case, most of you stick on the events and are miserable, like inhaling fumes throughout your journey

In the second case, you don't get permanent relief.

Because another bigger vehicle might come in front of you. Running away from events is not the permanent solution.

Wise people use their skill to surmount the event. If the vehicle is in perfect condition, the skill is perfect.

Conditioning the vehicle is practice and skill is the grace of guru.

THE WASHING MACHINE

Our body is like a washing machine. Our mind is like cloth. Love is like pure water. Knowledge is detergent. Each life time is one wash cycle. The mind comes into the body to get cleansed and pure. But if you put in mud instead of detergent, your clothes become dirtier than before. You will have to go on putting your clothes in the washing machine to get them cleaned. And the process repeats again and again.

Similarly you will have many more births until you stop repeating mistakes you have made.

Karma is related to God. These actions may be those in a present life or in school in Indian traditions, possibly actions in their past lives. The law of karma operates independent of any deity or any process of divine judgment.

Knowledge sharpens our skills like reasoning and problem solving. A strong base of knowledge helps brain function more smoothly and effectively. We become smarter with the power of knowledge and solve problems more easily.

Can we increase our knowledge?

Reading is the most personal and classic way to gain knowledge. Books, articles, blogs, novels, newspapers, guides, etc., are all fascinating reading sources. Apart from these, reading skill is a cognitive aid that strengthens your mind's cognitive network and enhances it over time.